ANDREW MARTIN

Interior Design Review Volume 18

Perhaps no profession has been shaped so much by women as interior design. In the 19th century, decoration had been overseen by the male dominated upholstery retailers and cabinet makers. The result was the heavy, dark masculine interiors that we associate with the Victorian era.

In 1874, Agnes Garrett and her cousin Rhoda Garrett established the first interior design company in London. They became not just the best known women decorators of their age but also two of the most significant and articulate figures in the fight for women's rights. They were a remarkable family. Agnes' eldest sister was the first British woman to qualify as a doctor. The youngest sister, Millicent, was president of the National Union of Women's Suffrage from its foundation in 1897 to when the vote for women was finally secured in 1918.

Agnes' and Rhoda's book 'Suggestions for House Decoration in Painting, Woodwork and Furniture,' published in 1876, was a runaway best seller. Their belief in free thinking individualism embraced in concert design, political activism and its natural partner, independence in business.

In 1881 the English feminist, Mary Haweis wrote 'The Art of Decoration' and also challenged the formulaic approach of the status quo. She pronounced 'one of my strongest convictions, and one of the canons of good taste, is that our houses ought to represent our individual taste and habits'.

Edith Wharton was a friend of Henry James, Jean Cocteau and Theodore Roosevelt and was three times nominated for the Nobel Prize for Literature. In 1897 she wrote 'The Decoration of Houses' and she too railed against the design orthodoxy of the day.

But nobody had such a dramatic effect as Elsie de Wolf. Her light and airy decoration of the Colony Club on Madison Avenue in 1907 was a radical reimagination of how an interior could look with women at the centre. As she said 'It is the personality of the mistress that the home expresses. Men are forever guests in our homes.' Her extraordinary career brought a clientele that included Vanderbilts, Morgans, Rothschilds, Fricks and the Duke and Duchess of Windsor.

She also served as a nurse in the First World War, invented the Pink Lady Cocktail, was named best dressed woman in the world and was immortalised in a Cole Porter song.

The quest for light reached its apogee with Syrie Maugham. She was the daughter of Doctor Bernardo (founder of the children's homes), lover of Gordon Selfridge and the Prince of Wales and wife to both Henry Wellcome and Somerset Maugham.

Her creation of the all white room in 1927 has become legend.

It is no coincidence that all these iconic figures led fiercely independent private lives. Rejecting the patriarchal values of the 19th century, defining an aesthetic, parallel to the suffragette campaign, they laid the foundations of the feminist movement of the mid 20th century.

In 1915, 10 of the 127 interior decorators listed in the London Directory were women. Now 67% of all interior decorators are women.

The women designers included in this edition of the Andrew Martin Design Review are worthy successors to their illustrious and trail blazing predecessors.

Martin Waller

Paolo Moschino and Philip Vergeylen
for Nicholas Haslam

Paolo Moschino and Philip Vergeylen. Nicholas Haslam Ltd, London, UK. An award winning interior design company which comprises two retail showrooms in central London, a showroom at the Design Centre in Chelsea Harbour and an international trade office. Recent projects include a chalet in Verbier, a country home in New York and a Kensington apartment. Current work includes three central London townhouses, a private residence in Holland Park, a large country house in Gloucestershire and a Sussex farmhouse. Design philosophy: understand the client and be original.

Eric Kuster

Eric Kuster. Eric Kuster Metropolitan Luxury, The Netherlands. Recent projects include Nikki Beach resort Koh Samui, a luxury penthouse in Monaco as well as the official launch of the Eric Kuster Metropolitan Luxury furniture and textile collection. Current work includes a large residential villa in New York, an extraordinary villa on Ibiza and a reputed hotel restaurant of a 3* Michelin Chef in The Netherlands. Design philosophy: contrast is happiness.

Allison Paladino

Allison Paladino. Allison Paladino Interior Design, Jupiter, Florida, USA. Specialising in high end, award winning interiors, yachts and commercial design plus luxury home collections. Recent projects include a residence in Palm Beach, Florida, a mansion in Rye, NY and a residence in an exclusive sports club in Jupiter, Florida. Current work includes the main and guest house at a thoroughbred horse farm in Ocala plus multiple houses in the Bahamas and a water front estate in Palm Beach. Design philosophy: timeless design which realises the clients' vision.

Design MVW

Ming Xu & Virginie Moriette. Design MVW Co Ltd, China. Specialising in luxury architecture, interior design and furniture design worldwide. Current projects include a three storey office on The Bund, Shanghai, a five star resort hotel in Lijiang, a historic tourism city in Yunnan province and Shanghai Tang stores for China & abroad. Recent work includes Shanghai Tang Cathay Mansion in Shanghai, Giorgetti Furniture Collection and Yun Long Club in Xuzhou. Design philosophy: to balance function and aesthetic using pure lines, lively forms and elegant proportions.

45

Wan Fuchen

Wan Fuchen. Suzhou FuChen Design Studio, China. Work is high end, with an emphasis on hotels, schools, offices, clubs and villas. Recent projects include Changzhou Detan Hotel, Meizhuishi Exhibition Hall in Suzhou and Baisha Lake private villa in Suzhou. Current work includes Shang Linglong Private Villa in Suzhou, Suzhou Tongli Chinese restaurant and Suzhou Xinguang video centre. Design philosophy: to strive for sustainability.

Studio Hertrich &

Adnet

Marc Hertrich & Nicolas Adnet. Studio Hertrich & Adnet, Paris, France. Projects are worldwide, including hospitality, hotels, spas, restaurants and residential. Recent work includes the interior design of the Sofitel Casablanca Tour Blanche Hotel, Morocco, a contemporary renovation of the legendary '70's Agora Swiss Night Hotel in Lausanne and the luxury redesign of Club Med Guilin, China. Current work includes a contemporary styled luxury boutique hotel in Rabat, sumptuous lounges for a club and sports stadium in Paris and a Relais & Château domain in a vineyard in the South of France. Design philosophy: to dream and create, combining functionality and poetry.

Yu Feng

Yu Feng. Deve Build Interior Design Institution, Shenzhen, China. Specialising in the interior design of commercial and public spaces. Current projects include The Oriental Club in Shenzhen, a sales centre in Xinjiang, Urumqi and the company's office space in Shenzhen. Recent work includes the interior of a complex, a high end office building and a commercial plaza in Guangdong plus a club in Hainan. Design philosophy: to preserve traditional Chinese civil engineering whilst embracing modern space design.

Interior Design Philosophy

Jorge Cañete. Interior Design Philosophy, Switzerland. The company's signature is always in search of projects with a poetic dimension. Recent work includes Marie Ducaté's art exhibition in a castle, a mansion in Geneva and a chalet in Chamonix. Current projects include a villa in Capri, a contemporary art museum in Basel and a champagne bar in Paris. Design philosophy: to create personalised projects by analysing three sources of inspiration: the environment in which the project is set, the feeling inherent in the location and the client's own personality.

ONE DAY AFTER THE
PASSING OF ALL OUR
EGOS WE MIGHT
COME HOME AND
BECOME AGAIN LIKE
THE MOVEMENT OF
THE LEAVES MOVING
ALL TOGETHER WITH
ONE CLEAR SINGING
VOICE AS THE WIND
HITS THE TREES BUT
IT WILL BE A LONG
TIME FROM NOW

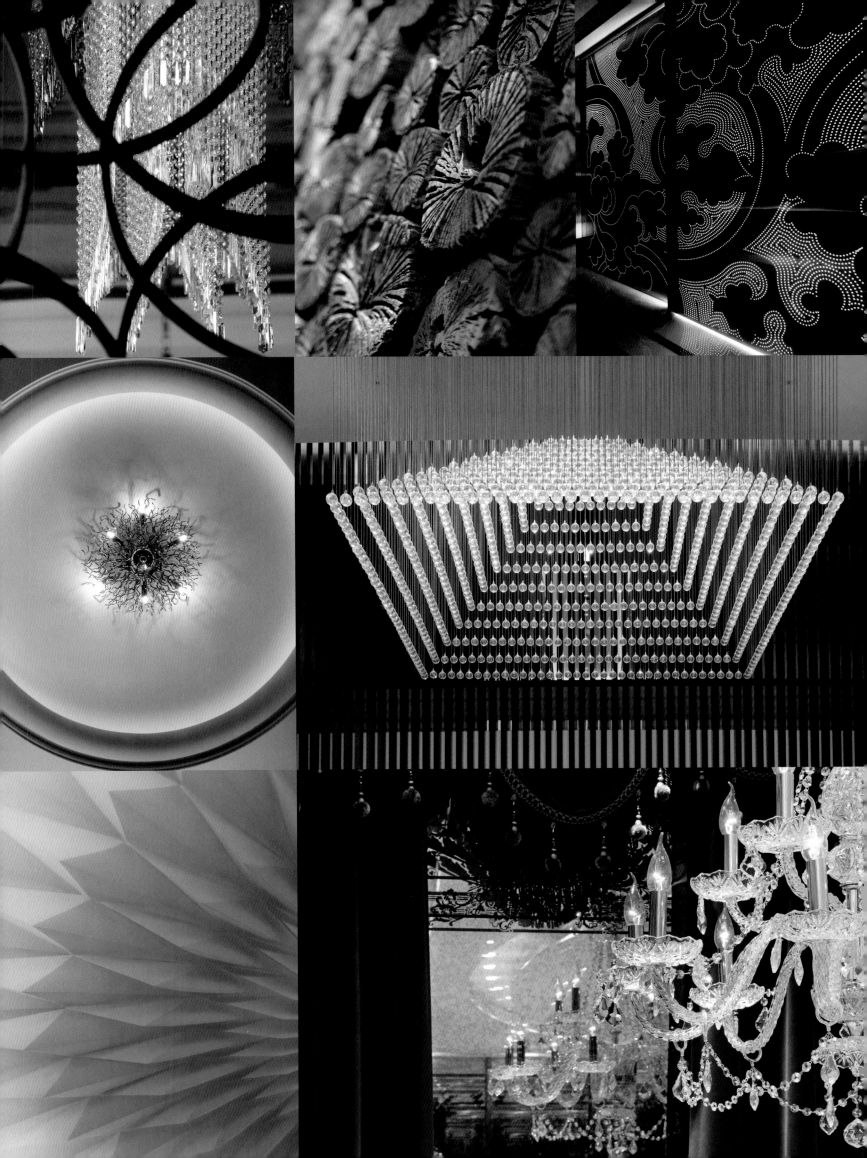

Sims Hilditch

Emma Sims Hilditch. Sims Hilditch, Gloucestershire, UK. A quintessentially British design practice, specialising in classic yet contemporary interiors for historic buildings as well as luxury residential and commercial properties. Current projects include the conversion of a 16th century pub into a contemporary design studio, a Cotswold manor house and a family mansion in Radlett. Recent work includes a house in Dorset, a Grade I listed crescent development in Bath and several luxury city apartments in London. Design philosophy: preserve authenticity, enhance character.

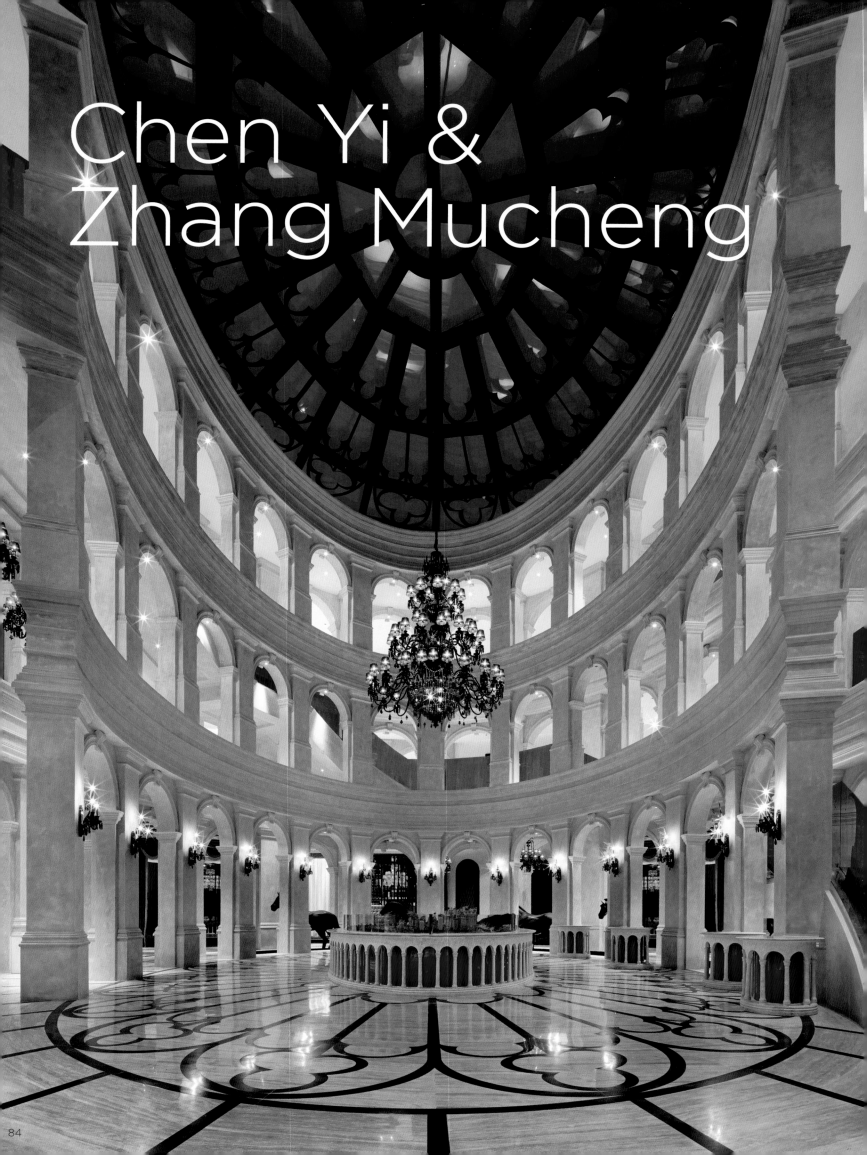

Chen Yi &
Zhang Mucheng

Chen Yi & Zhang Muchen. Beijing Fenghemuchen Space Design Centre, Beijing. Specialising in classic real estate, commercial projects, landscape and product design. Recent work includes a sales centre in Tianjin, a sales club design in Shenyang and another in Xining. Current projects include the architectural and interior design of Blue Lake restaurant and a club in Beijing, Lidu garden landscape design in Baoding industrial park and the showroom design of Tianjin Maple Blue International apartment. Design philosophy: to integrate art and culture.

Carl Emil Knox

Carl Emil Knox. Carl Emil Knox Design, Binningen, Switzerland. Established in 2005, the practice is increasingly sought after by an international clientele, specialising in building visual identities for offices, hotels, restaurants and public meeting places as well as creating home environments that reflect the values and personality of those who live there. Recent projects include a luxury estate in the South of France, a bachelor's apartment in Stockholm and a family home in London. Current work includes the offices for Scandinavia's leading model agency MIKAs in Malmö and Stockholm, a private holiday home in Southern Italy and a private residence in Basel, Switzerland. Design philosophy: art, simplicity and style.

Ben Wu

Ben Wu. W. Architectural Design Co, Shanghai, China. Specialising in hotels, clubs and private residences since 1993. Recent projects include Jiangshan 99 private villa in Ningbo and Beijing Cofco Auspicious Palace. Current work includes Sancha Lake Shimao centre sales office in Chengdu and Ningbo Fortune centre residential office apartment. Design philosophy: dedicated to forming a new design language with oriental philosophy and macro-aesthetic trend.

Yu-Lin Shin

Ligia Casanova

Nicky Dobree

Kunihide Oshinomi. k/o design studio, Tokyo. Covering residential interiors to skyscraper design in collaboration with professionals around the world. Current projects include a luxury duplex condominium interior next to the National Palace Museum in Taipei and a high rise penthouse interior in the centre of Tokyo. Recent work includes a campus project at a music college and several condominium interiors all in Tokyo. Design philosophy: to provide an amazing environment, through a wide range of design skills including landscape, architecture, interior and furniture.

Aleksandra Laska. Aleksandra Laska, Warsaw, Poland. An avid art collector, specialising in creating individual and timeless interiors. Recent work includes the partial remodeling of the National Opera House in Warsaw, a 1,700 sq m concrete showroom in Warsaw's city centre and a period apartment in Warsaw's old town. Current work includes a 130 sq m showroom located on Plac Dabrowskiego in Central Warsaw, a 70 sq m historic apartment and adjoining studio of painter Piotr Trzebinski and the renovation of a 1902 factory space in Moscow into a theatre. Design philosophy: to successfully combine contrasting elements.

Maria Barros

Maria Barros. Maria Barros Home, Cascais, Portugal. With a strong Palm Beach aesthetic, bold use of pattern and colour, Maria's influence stems from her time travelling and living in Florida as a teenager. Recent projects include a chic Lisbon family apartment, a fancy beach bar in the Lisbon coastal area and a holiday home in the Algarve. Current work includes redecorating a popular sushi restaurant in Cascais, a fashion boutique in Madrid and a family home in Alentejo. Design philosophy: making places that elevate the spirit. Promoting happiness through design.

Beijing Newsdays

Jianguo Liang, Wenqi Cai, Yiqun Wu, Junye Song, Zhenhua Luo, Chunkai Nie, Eryong Wang. Beijing Newsdays Architectural Design Co Ltd, China. High end commissions including hotels, clubhouses, restaurants, showrooms and public spaces. Recent work includes a renovation project for Wanliu Academy in Beijing, the Turandot Hotel and museums in Liling, Hunan Province and The Emperor Beijing, boutique hotel in Mudu. Design philosophy: serve the client with elegant solutions.

Honky

Hong Zhongxuan

Hong Zhongxuan. HHD Eastern Holiday International Design, Shenzhen, China. Pioneers in luxury and boutique hotels & resorts in China. Current projects include Modern Classic Hotel, Renhe Spring Hotel and Tianjin Light Hegu resort & spa. Recent work includes Beauty Crown 7 star Hotel in Sanya, Crowne Plaza Hotel Baoji and The Liuzhou Hotel in Shanghai. Design philosophy: functional, comfortable and elegant.

Angelos Angelopoulos. Angelos Angelopoulos Associates, Athens, Greece. Work is international, specialising in boutique hotels, private residences, apartments, restaurants, clubs, hotels, mountain & sea resorts, showrooms, workspaces, fabric design and conceptual design. Recent projects include a new beach resort in Cyprus, the architectural and interior design of a private estate in Athens and a private summer residence on a Greek island. Current work includes a restaurant in New York State, exclusive VIP villas at a beach resort in Cyprus and a private residence by the sea in Attica, Greece. Design philosophy: psychology and self expression.

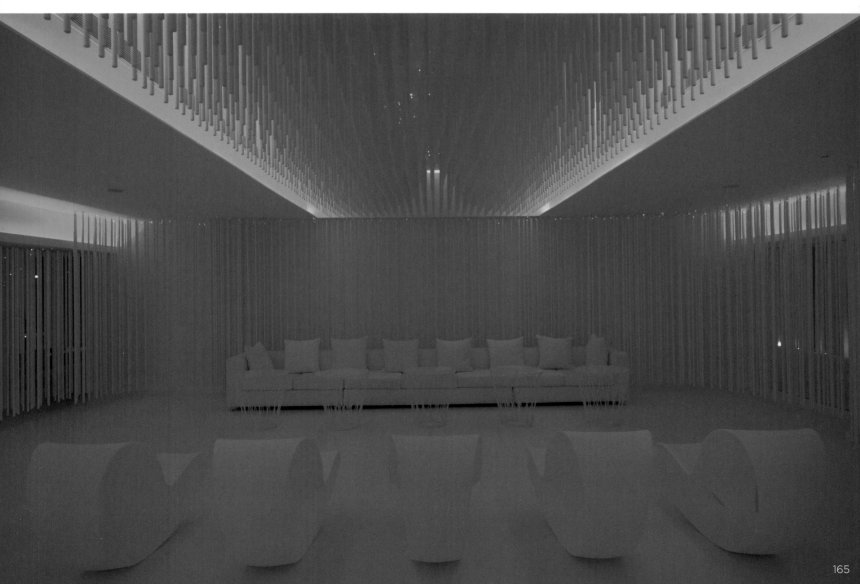

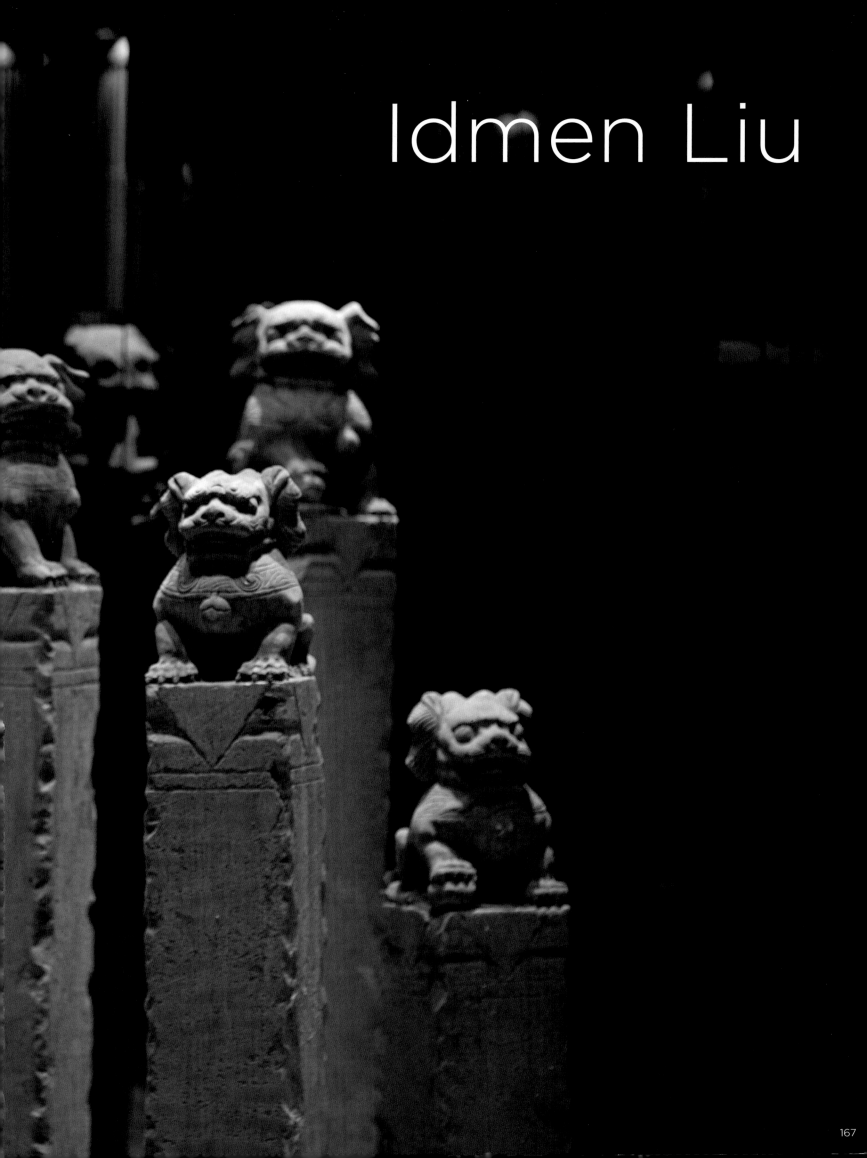

Idmen Liu

Idmen Liu. Shenzhen Juzhen Mingcui Design Co Ltd, Shenzhen, China. Dedicated to high-class and deluxe style interior design. Recent projects include Vanke Cheerful Bay Club House in Chongqing, Vanke City sales centre in Zhengzhou and Vanke Chengdu District office in Chengdu. Current projects include Wonders Ziyuntai Club House in Quanzhou, Tuo Ji Hong Bao Company office in Shenzhen and Vanke Jin Yu Xue Fu sales centre in Chongqing. Design philosophy: keep walking on the road of design.

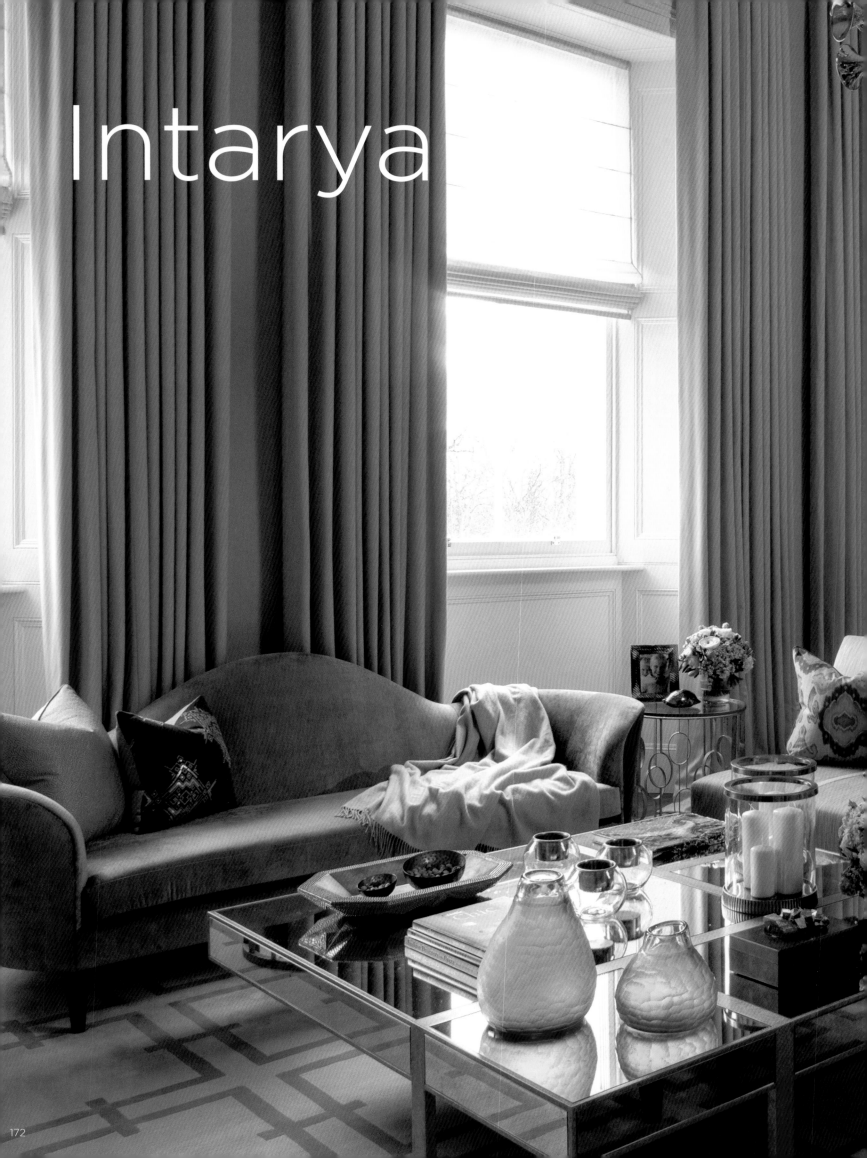

Intarya

Gu Teng

Gu Teng. Times Property Holdings Limited, Guangzhou, China. Specialising in real estate investment, development and management. Recent projects include Huangsheng sales centre in Guangzhou, Shidainanwan sales centre in Guangzhou and Shidaiqingcheng sales centre in Zhuhai. Current work includes Yunduan sales centre in Zhuhai, Times Experience Centre in Guangzhou and Xilong Living Club in Qingyuan. Design philosophy: to incorporate art with life.

AZULTIERRA

Toni Espuch. AZULTIERRA, Barcelona, Spain. Specialising in luxury residential and commercial interiors around the world. Current projects include a restaurant in Barcelona, the showroom of a major natural products brand and a luxury family house. Recent work includes Black Cocktail Bar, a high end home in Barcelona and a shop for a famous shoe brand. Design philosophy: to create warm, atmospheric spaces with character.

MPD London

THE DREAM FACTORY

Wmatter

anding
lts
alking.

d determined.

THE COACHING
INSTITUTE

ponsibilit

f the box think

el exc

nsatiable

learn and

Deliver

WOW.

fun with a little bit of quirk..

a sense of adventure.

Build a positive

am spirit.

race and drive

Intimate
Living
Interiors

Candy & Candy

Nick Candy. Candy & Candy, London, UK. Founded by Nick and Christian Candy in 1999, Candy & Candy is one of the world's leading interior design houses dedicated to designing the most luxurious real estate. Current projects include a Kensington penthouse, two properties in Cadogan Square, Knightsbridge and two further residences in Eaton Square. Recent work includes a five bedroom duplex penthouse with 360 degree views in Arlington Street, London, directly above The Wolseley restaurant and Cheval House, Knightsbridge a contemporary Art Déco styled five bedroom duplex penthouse. Design philosophy: driven by the pursuit of perfection.

Laura Brucco

Laura Brucco. Laura Brucco, Buenos Aires, Argentina. An interior architecture and design studio specialising in luxury residential, commercial and corporate interiors. Current projects include a villa in the most exclusive area in Buenos Aires as well as several large family houses. Recent work includes the interior architecture of a villa on the outskirts of the city, an impressive duplex for a tennis star and several flats in high end towers in the residential district. Design philosophy: timeless elegance.

Alejandro Niz &
Patricio Chauvet

Alejandro Niz & Patricio Chauvet. Niz + Chauvet Arquitectos, Mexico City. Established in 2002, specialising in a wide range of residential projects, restaurants and hotels. Recent work includes a private family home in Reforma Lomas, a hotel & spa in Arcos Bosques complex and a set of restaurants in the Santa Fe shopping centre, Mexico City. Current work includes projects for hotel developers, including Hotel Thompson in Playa del Carmen and the national hotel group Posadas. Design philosophy: functionality and comfort.

WORK HARD & BE NICE TO PEOPLE

TRENZSEATER

Ben & Hamish Lewis. TRENZSEATER, Christchurch, New Zealand. Specialising in high end luxury residential and commercial interior design both in New Zealand and internationally. Current work includes a French Chateau inspired country estate, an established grand home in Christchurch and several comprehensive large scale private residences around New Zealand. Recent projects include prestigious apartments in Auckland, Christchurch and Queenstown plus several high end private residences and holiday homes. Design philosophy: elegant and balanced.

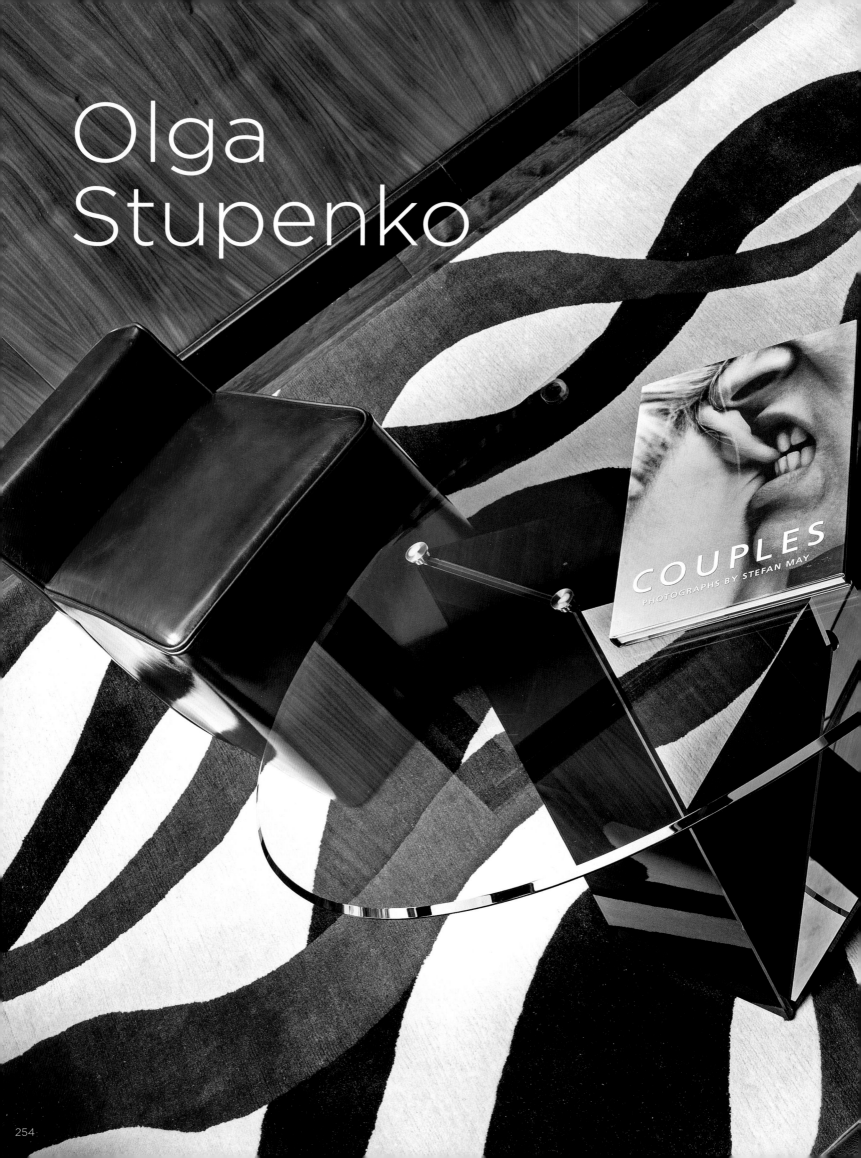

Olga
Stupenko

COUPLES
PHOTOGRAPHS BY STEFAN MAY

Olga Stupenko. Olga Stupenko Design, Oxfordshire UK & Moscow, Russia. Specialising in high end residential and commercial interior and architecture globally, with offices also in London and Monaco. Recent projects include several private mansions in Moscow. Current work includes a luxury hotel in France, a movie themed apartment in Moscow and a penthouse in Monaco. Design philosophy: to use simple shapes and proportions to create unique and timeless interiors.

Jiang Jianyu

Alexander James

Stacey Sibley. Alexander James Interior Design, Berkshire, UK. Delivering a complete service for luxury developers and high end residential clients. Recent projects include a landmark contemporary house in Surrey with views across three counties, apartments in Mayfair and Marbella and luxury hotels across Eastern Europe. Current work includes a residential refurbishment in Barbados, a large riverside house and a distinctive family home on the Wentworth Estate. Design philosophy: excellence and detail.

Suzanne Lovell

Suzanne Lovell, Suzanne Lovell Inc. Chicago, Illinois, USA. Luxury residential interior architecture, design and fine art. Recent projects include a private owner's suite at the St. Regis, Manhattan, a landmark Howard Van Doren Shaw penthouse on Chicago's Lakefront, a San Francisco Penthouse and Carmel Beachfront Estate. Current work includes an oceanfront penthouse in Miami, a villa in the South of France and a family estate in The Hague. Design philosophy: to create couture environments for extraordinary living.

Bo Li

Bo Li. Cimax Design Engineering, Shenzhen, China. A young team providing a variety of services including interior, architectural, exterior and product design. Recent projects include the renovation of a lakeside club, a private mansion and a villa show flat near the Lijiang River. Current work includes the landscape planning and interior for a high end villa community, the interior design for a large entertainment and sports club and the architectural and interior design for a seaside resort hotel. Design philosophy: focus on the user's experience.

Pippa
Paton

Tomoko Ikegai

Tomoko Ikegai. ikg inc, Tokyo, Japan. Established in 2006, ikg undertake a wide range of architectural and interior design services as well as the selection and coordination of art, furniture, electrical and household items. Recent projects include a poolside house for a family in Tokyo, a solar powered eco house and Matsukura Hebe Daikanyama clinic. Current work includes a commercial complex in Tokyo, a holiday home by the beach and the renovation of various residences. Design philosophy: to provide an environment to inspire and invigorate.

Julia Buckingham

Karen Akers

Karen Akers. Designed by Karen Akers, NSW Australia. A boutique practice specialising in residential design. Current projects include a heritage listed, Gothic style residence in inner Sydney, a beach front holiday house on the Central Coast of New South Wales and a heritage listed residence on Sydney harbor. Design philosophy: tailor made, combining new and old elements.

Kari Foster and design team Angie Pache, Jill Bosshart, Renee Keller, Rachel Blackburn, Michaela Jenkins, Jason Schleisman. Associates III Interior Design, Denver, Colorado, USA. Innovative responsible designers creating beautiful, healthy, and nurturing interiors for eco-conscious clients worldwide. Current projects include a modern family home in Vail, an Aspen Valley ranch and a flat in Houston. Recent work includes a California beach home, Colorado mountain retreat and a downtown Los Angeles hi-rise apartment, each a contemporary residence in which the interiors were a backdrop to the views. Design philosophy: inspiring change through environmental awareness.

Taylor Howes

Karen Howes. Taylor Howes Designs, London. An international interior design firm who have carved a niche in offering a luxury comprehensive design service to private clients, property developers & hoteliers. Current projects include a glamorous apartment in Grosvenor Square, a six storey townhouse in Kensington and an old rectory in Devon. Recent work includes a marketing suite for a well known developer on Berkeley Square, two show apartments in Mayfair's Jermyn Street and a sophisticated penthouse apartment in Chelsea. Design philosophy: to maintain creative excellence and friendly service.

Gloria Cortina, Vanessa Ocaña, Rafael Franco. Gloria Cortina Estudio, Mexico. A leading design studio specialising in city, country and beach homes to luxury retreats all over the world. Recent projects include a contemporary high-end residence set in a 4000 sq meter landscaped plot, a Mexico city apartment with panoramic views and Rancho LB, a multi acre country retreat. Current work includes Las Lomas, a home tailor made to display a collection of books and eclectic art pieces, Cabo 136 a beach house in Baja California, which showcases the company's first collection of beach furniture combined with Italian and Mexican fabrics. Design philosophy: signature concepts with the personality and textures of modern day Mexico.

Patrick Tyberghein. CarterTyberghein, London, UK. Specialising in luxury interior architecture in the UK and overseas including both primary and secondary private homes, residential developments and boutique hotels. Current projects include a villa in the South of France, a substantial seaside house in Jersey, major homes in Surrey and executive offices in Scotland. Recent work includes apartments in Hampstead, Regents Park and Kensington, a beach house in Barbados and a large family home in Wimbledon. Design philosophy: tailor made elegance.

Mona Hajj

Mona Hajj. Mona Hajj Interiors, Baltimore, USA. Focusing on high end residential and commercial projects globally. Recent work includes a waterfront condo in San Francisco, an interior and architectural renovation in Georgetown, DC and a horse farm in Kentucky. Current projects include a Beverly Hills villa, a period renovation in the historic Guilford area Baltimore and a farmhouse in Connecticut. Design philosophy: combine a global vision with an American emphasis on elegance, comfort and simplicity.

Oleg Klodt

Oleg Klodt & Anna Agapova. Architecture and Design by Oleg Klodt, Moscow, Russia. Bespoke interiors for residences and apartments in the luxury sector as well as projects for public buildings. Recent work includes an impressive home near Rublevskaya Highway, inspired by Soviet era Constructivism, a large Art Déco style apartment and a retail outlet for the French clothes company 'Loft design by...' Current projects include numerous large family homes in Moscow, a new meat themed restaurant and a range of Oleg Klodt designer furniture. Design philosophy: understated, harmonious, eclectic.

Jin Jian

Jin Jian. ZPSS. (Zhu Ping Shang She.) Hangzhou, China. Founded in 2009, ZPSS specialise in interior and furniture design. Recent projects include Zhupin coffee shop in Hangzhou, Guqiao restaurant in Chongqing and Shangshangting private villa in Hangzhou. Current work includes Shanghai boutique hotel, Moganshan resort hotel and Yangzhai private house in Nanjing. Design philosophy: art and design is for life.

Kamini Ezralow

Kamini Ezralow. Ezralow Design Ltd, London. A boutique design studio specialising in understated luxury residential and hospitality projects. Recent work includes a lateral apartment in the heart of Mayfair, a Swiss chalet and the refurbishment of guest rooms, suites and the outdoor space of the famed Marbella Club, inspired by the founders love of Californian living. Current projects include private residences in Dubai, a family house in London and a boutique hotel in Spain. Design philosophy: it's not just about environment, design from the inside.

Lanassir Lawes. Swank Interiors, Norfolk, UK. A residential and commercial interior design practise. Recent projects include an award winning restaurant in Norfolk, a New England style seafront home in Southwold and an apartment overlooking the marina in Ipswich. Current work includes a duplex penthouse apartment in Norwich, a grade II listed farmhouse in Norfolk and a barn conversion in rural Suffolk. Design philosophy: to enhance a building's architecture by fusing colour and texture.

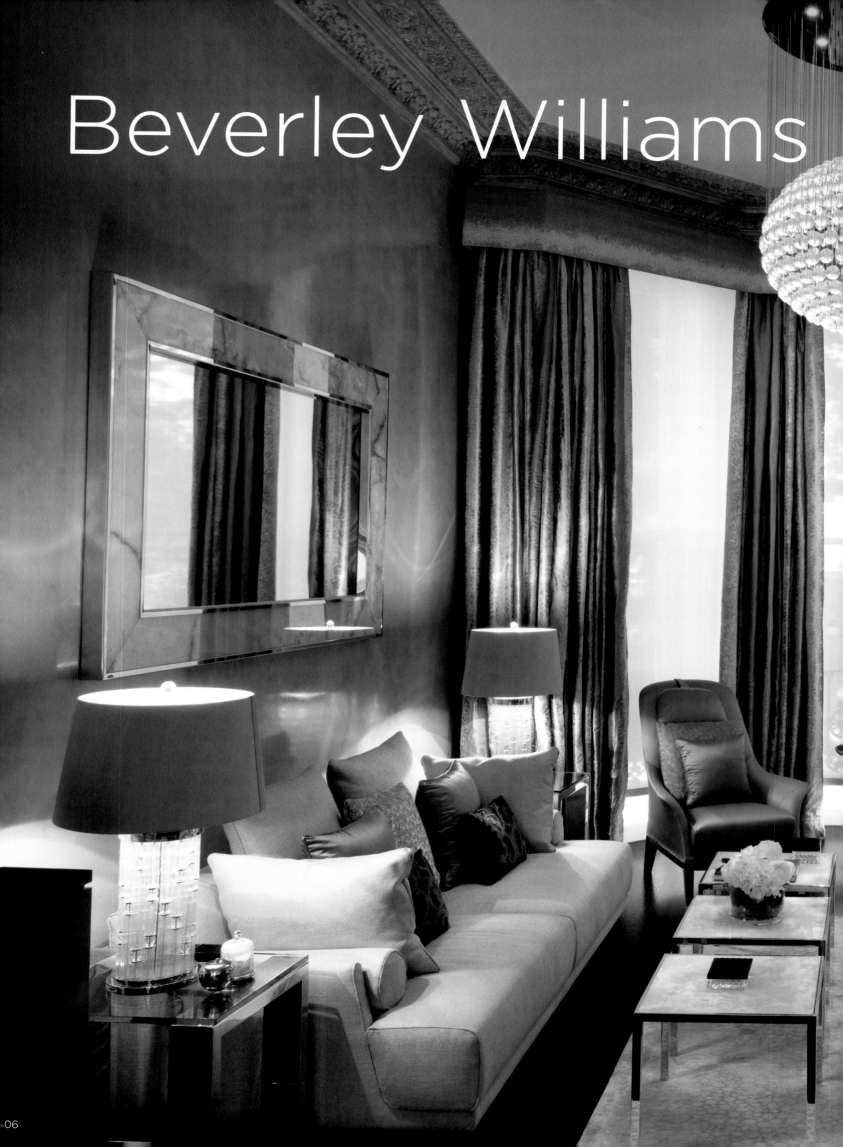

Beverley Williams

Elena Akimova &
Ekaterina Andreeva

Elena Akimova & Ekaterina Andreeva, Moscow, Russia. Working on a variety of projects from galleries to private luxury apartments and villas in Russia, Spain, France and Austria. Recent work includes scenography for the ArtBasel Fair 2013, the interior concept for Gallery 9/11 in Moscow, several private apartments in Moscow, their own exhibition space and scenography for the VIP lounge zone at Moscow Design Week 2010, 2011 and 2012. Current projects include a medical centre, two apartments in Vienna plus three apartments in Moscow and a villa in Ibiza. Design philosophy: can't live without humour and imagination.

METRO

IMPERIAL

&

LIKE THERE ARE NO WINNERS
GIVE
LIKE YOU HAVE PLENTY

ONE

Alexandra Schauer

Alexandra Schauer. Alischa Interior Design, Vienna, Austria. Work is international, specialising in custom made interiors, luxury chalets and private residences including hotels and castles. Recent work includes Hotel Stein in Salzburg, townhouses in Vienna, a chalet in Kitzbühel and a finca in Ibiza. Current projects include a series of residential projects in the mountains of Vienna, Salzburg and Tirol, the complete restoration of a villa in Munich, the renovation of a 400 sq m apartment in Moscow, an historic palace in Vienna, a lake house in Attersee and a private yacht in Italy. Design philosophy: harmony, luxury and comfort.

O

ABRAXAS

Christian Baumann. ABRAXAS Interieur, Zurich, Switzerland. Specialising in custom made, high end projects for an international clientele. Recent work includes interior design for a mountain apartment in Klosters, the complete interior design of the bar, meeting room and guestrooms in a boutique City Hotel in Winterthur and the concept

for two new apartments in one of the newest skyscrapers in the business district of Zurich. Current projects include a new build chalet in the Swiss mountains, a high end rooftop residence in downtown Zurich and a new build apartment in Lichtenstein. Design philosophy: designers are meant to be loved, not understood.

Matrix Design

Guan Wang, Jianhui Liu, Zhaobao Wang. Shenzhen Matrix I.D. China. Founded in early 2010 with a team of young and prominent designers. Recent works includes Chengdu Vanke Office, Jin Yu Ti Xiang Vacation Clubs in Sichuan Province and Zhengzhou Vanke Project sales centre. Current projects include Wandao Project sales centre in Wandao Real Estate, Yuewan Villa Show Flat in Chongqing and Model House of Shan Yu Qing Hui in Shenzhen. Design philosophy: to create a new world.

Tineke Triggs

Tineke Triggs. Artistic Designs for Living (ADL) San Francisco, California, USA. Specialising in luxury residential interior architecture and design. Current projects include a modern, high tech estate in Silicon Valley, a grand Victorian home in the exclusive Pacific Heights neighbourhood and a family retreat in the private community of Martis Camp, Lake Tahoe. Recent works includes a ranch in St. Helena, a private residence in Los Angeles and an artists retreat in Marin. Design philosophy: push the limits and break the rules to create unique spaces with enduring appeal.

GLAMOROUS

Yasumichi Morita. GLAMOROUS co. ltd, Tokyo, Japan. Established in 2000 the design office has since broadened its appeal to include projects in Hong Kong, Singapore, New York, London, Russia, Qatar and other major cities. Recent work includes B-one buffet restaurant at The Sherwood Taipei, Sunluxe Collection jewellery shop at One Central/MGM Macau and Galerie du Nord, bar in Osaka. Current projects include Morimoto South Beach Japanese restaurant at the Shelborne Wyndham Grand, Miami Beach, Isetan Shinjuku store renovation in Tokyo and a Baccarat chandelier to be displayed at Yebisu Garden Place, Tokyo in winter 2014. Design philosophy: glamour is key.

Designers
in the City

Christine Klein

Christine Klein. CKlein Properties, California, USA. Specialising in cost effective, eco friendly property renovation. Recent work includes the creation of Hammer and Nails Salon, the first for men only, on Melrose Avenue in Los Angeles, a Marina Del Rey penthouse, a glamorous laundry and powder room and the update of a West Los Angeles condominium. Current projects include an LA townhouse and a mid century West Hollywood penthouse. Design philosophy: to redesign energy efficient living spaces.

Editor Martin Waller
Project Executive Annika Bowman
Design by Graphicom Design

teNeues Publishing Group
Kempen
Berlin
London
Munich
New York
Paris

Production by Nele Jansen, teNeues
Editorial coordination Stephanie Rebel, teNeues
Colour separation by SPM Print

First published in 2014 by teNeues Media GmbH + Co. KG, Kempen

teNeues Media GmbH + Co. KG
Am Selder 37, 47906 Kempen, Germany
Phone: +49-(0)2152-916-0
Fax: +49-(0)2152-916-111
e-mail: books@teneues.com

Press department: Andrea Rehn
Phone: +49-(0)2152-916-202
e-mail: arehn@teneues.com

teNeues Digital Media GmbH
Kohlfurter Straße 41–43, 10999 Berlin, Germany
Phone: +49-(0)30-7007765-0

teNeues Publishing Company
7 West 18th Street, New York, NY 10011, USA
Phone: +1-212-627-9090
Fax: +1-212-627-9511

teNeues Publishing UK Ltd.
12 Ferndene Road, London SE24 0AQ, UK
Phone: +44-(0)20-3542-8997

teNeues France S.A.R.L
39, rue des Billets, 18250 Henrichemont, France
Phone: +33-(0)2-4826-9348
Fax: +33-(0)1-7072-3482

www.teneues.com

ISBN 978-3-8327-9863-5
Library of Congress Control Number: 2014942949
Printed in Belgium

Acknowledgments

The author and publisher wish to thank all the owners and designers of the projects featured in this book.

They also thank the following photographers:

Simon Upton, Clive Nichols, Gemma Miller, Paolo Moschino, Richard Monsieurs, Ron Blunt, Valentine Harmsen, Richard Powers, Kim Sargent – Sargent Architectural Photography, Copyright@Design MVW, Stian Broch, Pan Yu Feng, Xiangyu Sun, Antoine Baralhe, Alan Keohane, Fassbind Hotels, Chookia NG, L'Instant d'Or, Claude Weber, Qi Ma, Jenni Hare, Nicholas Watt, Gaelle Le Boulicaut, Eric Rakotomalala, Dany Savary, Liu Chun-Chieh, Polly Eltes, Xiangyu Sun, Johan Carlson, Ben Wu, Giorgio Baroni, Liu Chun-Chien, Ana Paula Carvalho, Philip Vile, Atsushi Nakamichi at Nacása & Partners Inc., Aleksandra Laska, Teresa Aires, She Wentao, Patrick Steel, Anson Smart, Chen Zhong, Jing Xufeng, Vangelis Paterakis @ studio paterakis, Costas Mitropoulos, Idmen Liu, Richard Waite, Mona Gundersen, Maria Bastos Vasconcelos, Montse Garriga Grau, Sascha Schulz, Carlos Vasconcelos e Sa, Gu Teng, Vicente Nebot, Joan Guillamat, Jake Fitzjones, Russ Kientsch, Mark Luscombe-Whyte, Ray Main, Estelle Judah photography, Carlos Ramos, Francisco de Almeida Dias, Peter Tjahjadi, Brevin Blach, Julian Abrams, Ines Miguens, Daniela Mac Adden, Adela Aldama, Joseph Sy, Patricia Madrigal, Karyn Millet, Andrew Bush, Hamish Lewis, Kirill Ovchinnikov, Jia Fang, Marc Berenguer, E House, Tony Mitchell Face Studios, David Shaw Photography, Jonathon Little, Andy Scott Photography, Rowan Chapman, Nick Ayliffe Square Feet UK Ltd, Tom Sullam, Eberle & Eisfeld, Toni Soluri, Billy Cunningham, Jessica Tampas, Vincent Zhang, Jianguo, Bo Li, Ted Yarwood, Matthew P. Wright, Jimmy Cohrssen, Akikio Amy Nakayama, Eric Hausman, Werner Straube, Vincent Zhang, Thomas Dalhoff, Scott Mc Gale, David O. Marlow, Gibeon Photography CO USA, Black Wang, Jerry Chao, Stacey van Berkel, Tom Sullam, Michael Calderwood, Chen Zhong, Patrick Tyberghein, Ajax Law Ling Kit, Jonathan Leijonhufvud, Scott Frances, Frank Herfort, Hans Fonk, Michael Stepanov, Jin Jian, Marcus Peel, Peter Bennett, Alexander James, Jeffrey Allen/ Jeffrey Allen photography, Isabelle Hay, Michail Stepanov, Jesus Alonso, Edina van der Wyck, Lufe Gomes, Maira Acayaba, Celia Weiss, Sylvaine Poitau, Zhao-min Kuo, Jo Ann Gamelo – Bernabe, Thierry Cardineau, Mikhail Stepanov, Charles Smith, Matt Livey, Olga Rubio, Markus Schauer, Marco Blessano, Frank Herfort, Maree Homer, Chenzhong, Eric Rorer, Philip Harvey, Seiryo Yamada, I. Susa, Jessica Lindsay, Nathan Worden, Nacása & Partners Inc.